Table of Contents

The Darkness and the Light
By Ismael S. Rodriguez Jr.

The Darkness and the Light / Ismael S. Rodriguez Jr.
2nd Edition
Copyright © 2012/2021 by Ismael S. Rodriguez Jr.

Ismael S Rodriguez Jr

365 NW 43rd CT
Oakland Park, FL 33309
ismael@bulletproofpoet.com

Dedicated to my muse and inspiration Maud Frainklen

1.0

Violent pacifists
The wild hunt begins
Peacefully killing
Sanctify hate
Vilification of true love
Painful release
Eternal damnation
Floating corpses bleed
Forlorn life
Blade cuts
Blood starts to flow
Salvation
Putrid flesh
The smell of sex
No more dreams
Thanatos take
Soul from flesh
Deliver me
Self-mutilation
Blood flows freely
Numbness ends
Lost dreams
Flowers in bloom
Nightshade
Ticklish prostitutes
Condoms in trashcans
Lost lives

A Song from Yesterday

Songs from yesterday
Dance on my tongue
Retrospection and dreams
Pictures from the past
Fall like autumn leaves
Manifested memories

A Thought

A thought entered my mind
It's just a little thought
Nothing much really
But I like it

ABC's of Purgatory

Absolution of my soul, in a swirling mass of colors
Brobdingnagian ravens peck at my eyes the answers begin to fade
faster than I can conceive
Confusing me for Thanatos, the ravens delight in my flesh and my eyes
those windows to my soul
Dogmatic revelations bind my spirit to purgatory, then angels
proclaim in
Eloquent speeches on my behalf, from the mass of the colors edge
Fathomless in content that mass of colors caresses me
Gehenna welcomes me as I drown in a river of angel tears
Hades oh Hades the infernal regions of my anima
Irrevocable sins stain my hands, erroneous lies told to myself
Justify and rationalize my descent into purgatory while the music of a
Klezmer echoes in my mind
Libertarians proclaim my innocence
Moralizing and rationalizing until nothing makes sense
No sequitur
Oblique in nature my obituary is read, disclosing my devotion to
Platonism, without answering any real
Questions, in fact it only raises more questions
Revealing the inconsistencies of my life
Slatrey eyeball a concept of my own nonsense, wrapped in
Tentacles of my own devising, tentacles forever
Undulating within my bowels, as I'm
Vehemently denying my downfall
While wandering through the lower pits of hell, where
Xenophobic behavior abounds, in dreams of
Yesterday's mistakes and majestic
Zither music cannot sooth my soul

Alone

Hello...
Hello...
Is anybody out there?
Anybody...
Please...
Someone...
Anyone...
I don't want to be alone
Not anymore

Black Friday Rules

It's only when I realize that my wisdom
Is only nonsense
That I touch the truth of wisdom
With divine dreams running through my mind
Utopia whispers sweetly
Into my ear

Cerebellum

Fearlessly ripping through
My own cerebellum
Grasping at the last remnants
Of my sanity
Diving headfirst into a sea of unreality
Fragmented voices
Still rage in my head
Like venomous serpents
Injecting their poison into my head
I'm trapped in my thoughts
With no way out
Destinies remorse
She cries for me
But the only one who can free me
Looks back at me through the looking glass

Columns

I open my mouth,
And words come out,
Where...
Do they come from?
Where...
Do they go?
I don't know what,
They mean.
So, I write them,
In columns.
To keep track,
Of them

Connected

I'm connected to something
Don't know what the hell it is
But I'm connected my friend
It tells me secrets
No one else knows
It's a voice I can hear
That no one else does
Whispering secrets into my ear

Craving Love

Craving love
Flesh on flesh
Bodies entwined
Slippery with sweat
Moaning...
Moaning...
Penetration...
Consuming fire

Creative Spunk

Damn I'm full of creative spunk
From start to finish
And every second in between
With pen or pencil
Brushes and paint
Soft or oil pastels
Conte crayons
Markers
Indian ink
Watercolor or acrylic
Oil paints too
Give me some paper
Or a canvas
I'll show you
That what I do
Damn sure ain't junk

Crystal Wishes

Multicolored wishes dancing in Kafkaesque landscapes
A whole other universe trapped
inside a small crystal box
A box that she keeps inside another
box
That one is a box made of jade
She keeps them both buried beneath a willow tree
One day just to see if wishes do come true
She dug up her box within another box
She took out the crystal one
Then walked to the lake
Where they say wishes are born
Holding her crystal box up to the sky
She watches as the sun filters
through
The sunlight comes out in little
rainbows
Each one more than the one before
Reflecting the universe trapped inside
Wondering how so much could be in a box so small
Then she puts her crystal box in her pocket
And dreams of her wishes to send them to the moon
As she touches the little box in her pocket and smiled to herself

Dance of Infinity

I think in infinity
Making my reality in dreamtime
Then dance on a pins head
With ten thousand angels
I soar with divinity
And drink nectar with the fey
Shoot lightning from my eyes
Then plant my roots deep within the earth
I make love with serenity
And draw from forces unseen
Then blend with the universe
And become an existential one

Dance of Slithering

Spiraling out
The dance of the serpents
A miniature cosmos
That caresses my soul
Grandiose gestures
In the writhing of snakes
Forked tongues flicker around
Tasting the air and each other
A musky scent drifts up to me
Then the rasping music
Of scales rubbing scales
Plays with my ears

Dances with Squirrels

I left the Pink Palace
The other day
And what
Did I see?
Rocky the squirrel
And all her friends
They were playing
And having lots of fun
So, I crossed the invisible bridge
It's a bridge that
Only goes one way
Then I sat beneath
The big pine tree
It's so big
That it even touches the sky
A sky that was
Bluer than any
Sky I'd seen before
sat on the crimson throne
Beneath the
Big...
Big...
Pine tree
Then watched as the squirrels
Danced their lives away
They took of
Their tails
And whirled
Them about
When suddenly sounds

Burst forth
Like no sounds I've heard before
So, I jumped off
The crimson throne
Then spun around to see
What was causing
Such a glorious ruckus
And to my surprise
What did I see?
There were chipmunks
Lined up in military precision
They jumped up and down
Then saluted each other
The next thing to happen
Was hard to believe
These chipmunks
They started to sing
And that song that they sung
Though I'd heard it before
Was a song
I could not remember
For it was in fact
None other than the forgotten song
Just as I thought
I'd witnessed all
To be seen
Racoons in grass skirts
Riding hornless unicorns
They suddenly appeared
Then joined with
The chipmunks
In sweet harmony

Then a great flock of birds
Roosting in the big pine tree
Did burst into the sky
Now it was time
For their fun to begin
They started to sing
An old melody
And my next big surprise
Was what was
Happening to me
My feet started tapping
In time with the beat
Then with energy
I didn't know I had
I began to dance
And sing along
Dancing to the Beat

Dancing to the beat of otherworldly drums

Forgetting dreams of tomorrows past
And foregoing the present for now
Dusty winds blow through my mind
Inventorying my memories
Of you and of me

Denied

I'm staring at this screen
And I don't know what to write
The muses have died in my heart
Ink still flows in my veins
But won't come out
Abandoned by my inspiration
No more words dance on my tongue
The only thing I have left
Is a deep emptiness in my soul

Desire

Forced evolution
There's no place to hide
Trapped in a void
With no place to rest
Absolution is still haunting me
The voices of angels
Flow through my head
Dear Kwan Yin
I call to you
With my cries of misery
They help me to fly
I compartmented my heart
So, I don't have to feel
Particles of psychotic dreams
Are keeping me alive

Divine Crown

Until the stars fall
My love for the divine
Faith walks a crooked line
Until I can no longer wear my crown

Fall

Fall
Then fly
Into dreams

Dogmatic Review

Filtered reality
The sum of true existence
Reflecting the truth
Without being true
A subconscious tribunal
The committee in my head
Facilitate thoughts
In an unknown way
Reality folds
In on itself
And freedom of
Enlightenment
Draws mysterious
Pictures
In the sand
That washes away
With the tide
And previous incarnations
Intrude on this life
I sanctify enlightenment
Until living is forgotten
And permeating yesterday
While freeing my downfall
And living without absolution
As my soul is dripping

Dream in Emotion

I dream in emotion
Full color 3-D feelings
Explode in my mind
With sounds and scents
While exploring my inner-being
And becoming more self-aware
I dream in emotion
They're bright and beautiful
And chaotic and serene
Dancing around in my mind
Secrets I want to share with you
As my heart drips through my pen

Dreaming Dreams

My dreams of dreams
They bring me to you
Your beauty
It encapsulates my soul
While our passion
Is encompassing all
And I fall into you
Then become whole
The emptiness in my soul
Only you can fill
But all of this
Is nothing more
Than an illusion
Just a dream of a dream
And sooner or later
I must wake up
And then you're gone
And I can no longer
Touch your soft skin
Or smell the sweet scent
Of your hair
Your lips are not mine to kiss
It seems like life it plays
This little game with me
By breaking my heart
When I realize
That you'll never be mine
I cry when I wake

For your love I'll never know
But when I sleep it
It brings a sweet release
For in my dreams
My dreams of you
I am yours forever
And you are mine too
There I can hold you close
And feel the caress
Of your soft touch
And breathe in the scent
Of your flowing hair
And taste the sweetness
Of your kisses
My desire for you
It causes both a pain
And a joy beyond belief
But though you may never be mine
In my dreams
My dreams of you
The light of our souls
They do combine

Dreams of Forever

I blow through the stratosphere
On an intergalactic mind trip
Rainbows of hyper-kinetic colors
Dance in the recesses of my mind
Time warps the never-ending story
And particles of psychotic dreams
Caress the inner-being of my soul
Dripping dreams of reality forever
Energy is swirling and endlessly spinning
Dancing the dance of all eternity
Then I'm falling down the rabbit hole
While angels sing forgotten songs

Dreams of our Hearts

Flowing words combine
And then a poem is born
The pain of the labor
Is outweighed by joy
Spinning carousels in the rain
On dragon back I ride
Floating
And remembering
The dreams
Of our hearts
It restores
The power
To the words
But don't dilute
Heal yourself
And
Heal
The
MOTHER

Dysfunctionally Literate

Have you ever known,
What you wanted to say
But didn't know how,
You should say it.
Do you ever think,
That your vocabulary was large?
Only to discover,
That you can't spell vocabulary
Does there, their, and they're,
Give you a great big headache?
Well my friend I feel that way too,
Or maybe that's two or maybe to
Have you ever wondered
Why "I" is capitalized? or why "a" is not "A"
And why is "be" or "bee" is not "B"?
I know what you're thinking
What's going on with this poet?
Is he literate or illiterate?
And just what the hell is this poem about
Let me tell you if I can
First of all, I believe
I'm Dysfunctionally illiterate
But I don't know what this poem is about

Elemental words

Words connect and form ideas
Then sentences flow into dreams
As real and unreal meld into one
Angels dance and fairies sing
We are born out of chaos
And into chaos we'll be free
Nature it answers questions unasked
Revealing beauty and the sublime
In every branch, leaf, bud, and flower
Elementals whisper their truth to us
As flowers bloom unheard and unseen
Love God's creature both great and small

An ending of an era

The things I have to say
The voices suggest caution
While a perfection
Of an ungodly sort
Points toward
An unnatural love

Enter the Mind

The flowing eddies
Of true delusions
Ring echoes
In my mind
We're floating
In dreams
Flowers
That bloom
Into vision
And internal bliss
Then slipping
Into unconsciousness

Epigram

Doors into nowhere
Open in my mind
Showing glimpses
Of yesterday's tomorrow
CHANGELESS
UNREACHABLE
Formless shapes in the mist
Sanctify my love
The words that I speak
Have lost all meaning
LIVE
LOVE
LEARN
Drowning in hope
And breathing in lust
Passion is a typewriter
Without any keys

Expounding the Mysteries

(Of Hypocrisy)

Nothing is self-evident
In a world full of lies
The greatest tradition
Of the world's religions
Is to love one another
And do no harm
Nothing is self-evident
In a world full of lies
Brother against brother
In an ocean of hate
The poor and helpless
Are the world's kicking dog
Nothing is self-evident
In a world full of lies
Individuality is forsaken
For a plastic mask
Freedoms are diminished
In the land of the free

Fates Little joke

I've become my own enemy
In my mind I want to die
It's the only way to escape from myself
And the wasteland of my life
Becoming what I hate
I'm just a creature of apathy
What is this cruel fate?
What meaning does my life have?
No longer can I fight it
For I lack the strength
To crawl back into the light
There is no will to continue this life
I'm rotting from the inside
And the pain is too much to bear
It's from myself that I want to hide
And walk away from this dismal life

Fear and the Self

I cut myself to feel
The numbness will not stop
I'm cold and alone
With no dreams in my heart
Abandoned by the light
My fears take control
Driving me deeper and deeper
Into the recesses of my mind
Terrified of the day
I prowl by moonlight
Alone and afraid
By myself I must fall

Filth of Flesh

Puss is draining from my rancid soul
Hating all but myself most of all
Slicing my flesh releases, me
Drowning in piss
Not cleansing the filth
Masturbating in a morgue
Nocturnal emissions
Tell me the truth
And I can't live knowing that
Dying on the inside
The façade finally falls
I can no longer be
Something I'm not
I wish I could love
But I can't even feel
This lack of emotions
It always taunts me
The pain in my flesh
Is all that keeps me alive
Forsaken and alone

Floating in a Sea

Floating in a sea
Of multicolored dreams
Memories capture illusions
Of forgotten pasts
Forsaken and alone
Yearning to be touched
But nobody can
Even see who I am
Love has abandoned me
In this purgatory
I must dwell alone

Flow

Ripples below
The surface
Of my mind
Are carried away
By eddies of thought
Through the past
And into the present
Then dreams
Of futures
Yet to come
Distract me
Before another
Whirlpool of emotions
Pulls me under

Floating on Dreams of Yesterday

Floating on dreams of yesterday
Mix with the reality of tomorrow
Then euphoria climbs
To unexpected heights
Partake of the folly
While breathing in the soul of Geb
And drinking the juice of forbidden melancholy

Forgotten

I've forgotten myself
In dreams of tomorrow
How can I find myself
In this ocean of pain?
I don't even know
Where the hell I am
I can't move forward
With all these walls
I've built around myself
What I once thought
Was my only protection
Is crushing the life
Right out of me
So, BRICK by BRICK
These walls I've
Must come down now
Please forgive me
For all I've done to you
But how can I love you
When I don't even
Love myself
But now I know
This cycle of self-loathing
Has to come to an end
But through it all
I've forgotten
Who I am

Free Dumb

Free but dumb
In today's modern society
IQ's have fallen
But we can tweet
What we want
Screw any real news
Give me celebrity gossip
And conspiracy theories
America's heartland
Land of the free
And crystal meth labs
Time to fear everyone
Who isn't like me
America first
A vanilla culture
That's as bland as it's free
We don't need any laws
Everyone follows
The same
Goddamned trends

Free Form Love Affair

How much do I love you?
Let me count the ways
1,2,3,4,5,6,7,8,9
And sometimes even 10
I think love is a glandular problem
Especially the pituitary gland
It all stems from the God particle
Or is it the God forsaken one

Freedom of Muse

Draining from my head
Is a constant flow
Of words
And images
Fly freedom fly
The muse
It's in me
Be a light unto
YOURSELF
I must write
The paper
It calls me
So how
Do I
Get it out
It just keeps
Flowing
While colors
Dance in my heart
Forms
And shapes
Sing to me
I'm floating on
A natural high
Of emotions
And surges
Of the things to come
And then
BANG
I explode

Into joy
All over again

Freedom

Freedom clings
To the soul of man
Reaching deep
Into his core
It's buried deep
In the heart of love
And strives to grow
Beyond all dreams
When guided by love
And the sacred divine
Freedom grows
To touch us all

Fruit of the Gods

Grasping at straws
To taste the forbidden fruit
It's as sweet as sin
But the aftertaste is bitter
Reminiscent of ambrosia
The flavors dance on my tongue
Flawed in its perfection
The fruit of the gods
Consumes the consumer

Gifts of Wisdom

The heavens shower down gifts
On those ready to receive them
Like a gentle rain soothing the soul
We receive these gifts that cannot be seen
The wind blowing through the leaves
Teaches us lessons of the balance of life
Whispering truth to those who can hear
The wisdom of Gaia the mother of all
Stars chart courses of life unseen
Written in the sky for all to read
The twelve prophets of the zodiac
And the planets they receive
We have plants and herbs to soothe and heal
The magick of the ages in stem, leaf, and bud
A brew for the tongue and incense for the nose
Mixed and combined with the powers of earth

Hold Me

I've come to a decision
What I'm going to do
Is slather my crotch
With peanut butter
Then put squirrels in my pants
Then scream at people
Tell them what I think of them
Tell them the truth
Then pull a squirrel out of my pants
And make them eat it

Holding the End

My euphoria has ended
And bliss has dissolved
Portraits lay unfinished
The brushes
Have all been broken
The paint
Has run out
The visions I breathe
Are now crushing me
Only the outside
Has been polished
The inside is rotting
And all growth
Has become stagnant
A stream flows in
But no longer flows out
I've become trapped
And rancid
Like a disease
My dreams have all died
And love is forsaken
The emptiness inside
Erodes my self-will
I'm chilled to the bone
And the sun in the sky
It no longer
Warms my icy soul
Barren and unloved
This final decent
Into the hell

Inside my mind
I'll be forsaken and broken
Until the day I die

I Ain't Speaking

I call myself crafty sometimes
But that's only
In my off moments you see
The moments I live and breathe
And sometimes piss out art
A hot stream of creativity
That explodes from deep within me
But these moments are fleeting
At least I think they are
Maybe just maybe they ain't
But really, I don't care
I live foe those moments
That's all that I know
When there's a fire
Raging inside my gut
That my brain can't contain
And what's hidden inside
Suddenly bursts forth
It's like some damn verbal diarrhea
The tension just builds
Until it must come out
Then I start shouting words
That I don't understand
Maybe these words come
From some different reality
Where they make fucking sense
They sure as hell
Don't belong in this world
But these words in me
I keep spewing them out

I don't know how the hell
I can stop them at all
So, I just call it art
Yeah, that's a good name for it
It might be a poem or a little prose
But spoken word that ain't shit
I scream my damn words out
Because you don't want to hear
So, I piss my damn art
All over your shoes

I Can't Write

I joined this website recently
It said for serious writers only
Now there's a question
I just have to ask
Can I really
And I mean really write
Now this happens to be
A very difficult question
I must ask myself
I've got these voices in my head
Degrading my self-esteem
And there are times that I feel
As if there's nothing I can do
But the answer I must know
And so, I will try
So, I take out my notebook
And my favorite pen
Now what do I write?
I really don't know
And the blank page
That's in front of me
It torments and tortures my soul
And the voices in my head
Start laughing sarcastically
Then they ask me
"Just who the hell
Do you think
You're going to fool
What makes you think
You can write anything at all?

You're just a big joke
And that's all you'll be"
But if I'm to know
Shouldn't I at least give it a try
The voices of self-doubt
They have this to say
"Give up now"
I don't pay attention
To these self-defeating voices
That are inside of me
Instead I'll imagine
Of the great things I'll write
I'll think of all the people
Who'll devour every single word
They'll feel everything
That I put on the page
And then they'll know
My joy and my pain
But the only thing I can do
Is stare at this page in front of me
It's still blank without any words
And staring right into my soul
The voices of uncertainty
Still laugh and scream inside my head
They're still taunting and screaming
"Look at the paper you fool
There not a thing on it
And there never will be"
Maybe it's time for a break now
I could watch some TV
Or read a good book
It's definitely time for some coffee

And time for a smoke
I know that I can't put this off
At least not for very much longer
It's time that I must
Get back to my dream
I know I can do it
I just need to try
So, I take out a dictionary
And a good thesaurus too
They're filled with great words
My heart yearns to use
But something is missing
No matter how hard I try
I don't know how to take these words
And put them together for you to read
The voices still laughing in my head
Screaming louder than before
"Didn't we tell you there's nothing
You can do you idiot
You're a pathetic joke
And that's all you'll be"
Could these voices in my head
The ones I hate most
Screaming and laughing
And call me stupid be right?
What if it's really true?
Everything that they say
How can they know?
It can't be true
THAT I CAN'T WRITE!

In My Dreams

Falling down
Pit of despair
My new happy place
Grovel in shit
Dance to the funeral march
Blade in my flesh
Cleanses me
Blood flows out
Taking my sins with it
The pain of my body
It lets me feel
The hurt and sorrow
Deep inside of me
Tattooed flesh
Suffer and bleed
Self-mutilation
Salvation for me

Infinity

The smallest slice of infinity
Is still infinity too
Then there's this question
I once asked a teacher
"If the universe is infinite
And the universe is expanding
Just where in the hell
Is it expanding to?"

It Would Suck

(To be on the winning side of dying)

Great Holy Mother
Help me please
To release the pain
The bane of my heart
I just want to feel
Some of the joy

Ja Na Sais Quoi

Permanent metamorphosis
When will it change?
Ja Na Sais Quoi

Jaundice

Acceleration of gravity forces me to
Become what I don't want to be
Conscious of my unnatural
Desires for you and
Everything you stand for
Forgive me Father for I am sin
Gratification of my flesh
Hinders my intentions
Just as macabre dreams
Kill my soul
Letting another piece
Of my love die
Morbidly in pain
Necrosis of my heart like an
Open and festering
Puss dripping wound
Quarantining my soul
Rancid as it
Serendipitous actions
Tempting me into
Unadvisable positions
Validating the
Wanderlust in me as
Xenophobic natives
Yield to
Zero

Just a Little Fun

Right from the start
I've got to say
This is nothing serious
I'm just having a little fun
I've danced with squirrels
Sang forgotten tunes
This may seem
A bit frivolous to some
But as I've said
It's just a little fun
I've been kissed
By the moon
And drank
The morning dew
I don't really know
If I'm making any sense
All I know is this
I'm having a little fun

Oblique

Haunted by drug dreams
The only way home is gone
Performing strange rites

Karmic Retribution

I'm spending another birthday
Locked up in the bug house
Why do they try to fix me?
Don't they know
There's nothing wrong
With my mind at all
Just put a stop
To all this therapy
And don't try to give me ECT
However, it's not really
All that bad actually
Being kept locked in here
They keep giving me
Lots of colorful pills
To keep me sane
It makes me content
To take all these pills
That kill my head
But what makes me most happy
I know that one day
I'll be off the suicide watch

Litost

Hahaha
You've fallen again
Suffer like always
Look in the mirror
Forget who you are

Little Timmy's Happy Place

In little Timmy's happy place
He's making his plans
To kill all of us
He wants to destroy humanity
He has lots of guns
To make holes in your head
Then he'll start laughing
When your brains fall out
Carnage gives him a boner
And he baths in human blood
He likes to eat the flesh of man
All the women he loves are all dead
He wants to make earth a hell
Death is his only master
And he follows his calling
To bring death and misery
Visions of massacres bring him joy
Machetes hacking into flesh
And hammers bashing skulls
Are glorious to little Timmy

Little Timmy's Summer Vacation

Little Timmy's off work
All of the week
It's summertime
Let the vacation fun begin
Little Timmy
He likes to go to the Jersey shore
And when he arrives
He gets wasted
He goes on vacation
In his special van
The one he calls
His death machine
He fills it with
His lovely toys
All of his favorite guns
He also takes
Some sharp knives, hatchets
And machetes
To slice and chop
The people he meets
Plus a few blunt objects
To bash in skulls
As he drives around
And picks up hitchhikers
And that my friend
Is when real fun
Really begins

Look

STOP LOOKING AT ME
No wait a minute
I want you to look at me
Please let me be noticed
Without being seen
I crave your love
But fear your attention
Look at me
Stop looking at me

Lunar Queen

Moon light shines down on my path
Will it show the way?
Please my lunar queen
Show me the way
To honor you
Maiden your gentle touch
Stirs my passion
Mother of all
Provider and nurturer
In you bosom I weep
Crone you complete the cycle
Wise one dark one
In the end I come to you
Hear me Goddess
As I cry for your help
Show me the way
The way to the truth
The way to be at one with all
To see the wisdom
In every rain drop

Mass Illusion

Pacified drones
Eating the
Hell, out of the
American dream
Mass illusion
The zombies tremble
Drowning in a sea
Conformity
Self-deceit
Joy the drug
Keep them happy
The new fall
Schedule
How many served now
Biotechnology
The new breadbasket
Headless chickens
Legless cows
Nothing can be
Different
We must
All
BLEND
Gnostic words
Pagan hopes
Atheist faith
Sacred and
Divine
In all
Diversity

Mom

Mom...mom...
How can I tell you
How sorry I am?
I stole from you
That weighs so heavy
On my heart
I tried to do my best
With this monkey
On my back
But the truth mom
I rarely told
You took care of me
In my times of need
Did I look like a good son?
When I took care of you
Mom...mom...
I can't even imagine
How you felt
What you went through
When the biopsy said cancer
But you showed a strength
Beyond anything I knew

Mystery Unfolds

Dance the dream under the moon
Energy vibrates to its own frequency
Divinity and self-merge into one
Marking the transition
To higher self-consciousness
Listen to the whisper in the breeze
Gentle answers to all mysteries
Drowned out by sorrow
And voices screaming to be free
Dare to compare self to self
Yesterday to today
Be aware of the now

Night Sweats

Woke up
In a cold sweat again
Theses nightmares
Are killing me
I grab for her hand
But her fingers
Slip from my grasp
Then flames rise
And consume her
No wait
'm thirteen again
Tying a rope
Around my neck
Then I see him
Gun at his head
I scream NO!
Don't do it
But he pulls the trigger
That's when I wake up
SCREAMING

No More

How many times
Do I have to say?
"You're not
Supposed to love me"
Why don't you hate me?
Everyone else does
Why not you?
I've hurt you
And lied
Then turned
My back on you
Again, and again
But still you insist
That it's me you love
A love I don't know
If I can return
How can I love you
With a heart
That has died?

Numb

Blade slicing wrist
I begin to feel
Numbness slips away
When my flesh
Starts to bleed
Protecting myself
From whatever is real
The particle dreams
Are starting to flow
Life within life
Blood holds me together
I open my mouth
But nothing comes out

Ode to a Soup Kitchen

Most days... the food...
I eat...
comes from...people who...
don't know me...
without their generosity...
how would I eat...
or would... I just starve...
if not for the...
line to...
the soup kitchen...
door...
what hope I...
have...
may soon...
be...
no more...

Old Shoes

My shoes are old
With holes in the soles
They're falling apart
I've walked to many miles
With these shoes
Endlessly
Day and night
With no place to rest

One More Time

Another morning waking up in a shelter
How did I get HERE once again?
Does it really matter how?
Do I need to find out why?
Or should I try one more time
To make what's left
Of my life
Into a life better?
I did it before
Let's see if I can do
It better
This time

One

Extraterrestrial astral projection
Alien Buddhists caring
For the universal enlightenment
Pieces of reality melt
Filling empty spaces
With nothing
Phased out of focus
Exist for dreams
The only thing
Worth living for
Disconnected thought
Blend with illusion
Creating the
New form
Patterns sparkle
Mandating the urge
Developing into
The
One

Origami Boxes

With paper in different
Sizes
Colors
Patterns
A couple foil ones too
I make origami boxes
All different kinds
The shapes that I make
They are
Squares
Triangles
Hexagons
Octagons
And some kind of look like
Japanese lamps
Some of the paper boxes
I make they have other
Things placed on top
Flowers
Hearts
Birds
And butterflies too
Into these boxes I make
I place within them
All my
Love
Joy
And hope
It's like I made me
A new heart out of paper

Pacified Order

Welcome to the new world
The world of verbal regurgitation
Where everyone is bored
In this dying wordless nation
The dream has died
For us pathetic little fools
To us hope has lied
Nothing is left we are tools
The new world order
Of violent pacification
Trapped on the wrong side of the border
In a morbid confrontation
The tears that I have cried
For the hope we have lost
Now that my tears have dried
I wonder, was it worth the cost

Paradise

Every time I look at you
My heart sinks into a hole
I know your love
Will never be mine
No matter how much
I love you
To you I'm just a friend
And that's
All I'll ever be
But to me
You are like
My earthly paradise
And I will never taste
Your forbidden fruit

Paper Cranes

paper cranes
they make
me dream of how
things could have
been
fluttering around
in the wind
a multicolored
dance
of paper
one
thousand
little dreams
lifting me up
making
me cry

Paradox and Answers

I've been told by some people I know
That I ask some interesting questions
The answer my friend is very easy to see
I want to learn all that I can
How do I know what's relevant to me?
Unless I give it a try
How do you do this?
How do you do that?
What do you think about stuff?
To learn all I can and continue to learn
I must be open to all knowledge
Questions of life and death
Of joy and sorrow
My mind enjoys the paradox of it all

Particle Dreams

Particle dreams
Flow through my mind
Both here and there
And then beyond
Voices they whisper
The secrets of ages
And tell me lies
But particle dreams
They keep me sane
Showing past and present
And glimpses of tomorrow

Peanut Poem

Peanuts: stanza I
Peanuts
Peanuts
almost a pea
not quite a nut

peanuts: stanza II
Peanuts
Peanuts
goobers peas
I like how you taste
and your good for me
peanuts: stanza III
This one ends as the first two start
I like to eat them all kind of ways
In truth I think they are a great little snack
and now comes the time for
the last stanza to end
peanuts
peanuts

Poppy Tea

Skin crawls
While the nausea builds
Just a sip...a little sip
To satisfy my soul
And make me complete
One little sip
Is all it'll take

Questions Only Questions

The name of the game
Is to answer the question of self
What is my true will and where will I go with it?
Questions of longing beg to be answered
Look deep for the answers
Be fearless and thorough
And leave no stone unturned
Cross the abyss my friend
That mirrors the darkness inside of you
Revealing both your flaws
And divinity within you
Dance and dream
Then answer questions unasked
The truth you seek is plain to see
But obscured from sight
Behind the ego of self

Rain

Drip
I Drip
Drip
Water drips from my hat
I'm cold and wet
Still I stand
In the rain
Shivering
So cold
So cold
The rain pours down
And I stand in it

Reflection

I stand at the last abyss
That mirrors what's in my soul
It reflects the dark abyss
That lives inside of me
Then change the angle
We're permeating realities
But the reflection stays the same

Skulls and Bones

I dream about skulls
But I do like the feeling
Skulls and bones skulls and bones
Dancing in my mind
I'm singing in the moonlight
Surrounded by my skulls
Skulls and bones skulls and bones
Dancing in my mind
Darkened paths for me to take
Wandering through the night
Skulls and bones skulls and bones
Dancing in my mind

Slatrey Eyeball

my left eyeball
was watering today
it's because I'm easy
you better believe
I rode a dog
till the cats came home
Then a sign
of the lime
that showed my crime
was used to spank time
uber giants came to me
stole my lime sign
so, I put ferrets
in my pants

Starlight Magick

Dancing in starlight
And drinking in the moon
Fauns and nymphs
The precious ones
They're celebrating joy
Frolicking and playing games
Of a forgotten time
The mead it flows
In abundant streams
From fairy mound to fairy mound
The grandest ball you ever did see
Trapped inside the fairy circle
The magick starts to grow
Call upon the power of the Goddess
In perfect love of course

Techno Love

Joy and passion
The beginning of all
Text my heart to
Your latest blog
Warmth form my soul
I send to you
Passion and joy
The end doesn't come
Reach out and touch another
Twitter and SnapChat
Send out my digital love
Taste my technological lust
Freedom is the key
But its action that
Opens the door
www.thetearsicry.luv
I cry for the loves that I lost
And for the love I will never know

Testify the Open Road

A 33% solution
Filled with paranoid dreams
As fantasies bite my ankles

The Awakening

Awakening to a new beginning
The emotional overload
Has finally ended
Beneath what wasn't
I come face to face with me

The candle Burns

The candle burns
Brighter and brighter
Casting a light
That diminishes the dark
Bask in the warm glow
Of the candles flame
While blooming and growing
And reaching for the light

The Darkness and the Light

In the dark I dwelled for too long
Afraid that the light would burn my eyes
Driven by lust but longing for love
And spiraling down a pit of despair
The darkness enclosed all of me
And fear was the force driving me
Forcing me into a great depression
Blinding my sight to thing of the light
This darkness fen on my fears
Burrowing deep into my soul
But now in the light I rejoice
A candle whose flame has grown
And now encompasses my life
Twirling and jumping in a dance of joy
Growing before the lady of the night
The light of the sun reflected on the moon
Lighting the path for me
And pulling my soul to greater heights
Filling me with a growing love
And opening my eyes to the beauty in all

The Heart of my Craft

The heart of my craft
Is in its ability to tell a story
Its soul is its ability to touch a heart
Before anything else that's my goal
To tell a story only I can tell
To make you cry then make you laugh
The story I tell is filtered through my mind
But it starts in a place deep in me
A place full of emotions
From heart to head
Then it bursts through my hand
As they caress this keyboard
Like it's my one true love
But if the truth should be known
Words are my real love
The words that flow from me to you

The Passion of Love

Freedoms release,
Is trapped in the past.
Pandora is truly,
The gift of all.
A box of ills,
Curiosity opened.
Hope is all that's left inside.
The Olympians rejoice,
The courage of love.
It took so many incarnations,
But did I finally get it right.
So many loves that I have lost.
I'm no longer sure,
If my heart will ever heal again.
Aphrodite whispers in my ear.
Love is the start,
That goes to the end.
Passion and lust a gift to all.
The feeling the Goddess gave to me.
They feel trapped inside,
Like fossils in amber until, time stands still.
The Graces and Muses,
They sing to me.
Queens of Song, the joy inside.
Takes me up into the sky.
I am the cloud and the cloud is I.
The love that I feel,
Awakens my heart.
My life sweet love,
From birth to death.

And all between.
Look
At
The
Box
With hope inside.

The truth About Bad Dreams

The moon

Is my guide

On this dark

And dismal night

Around every

Bend in

the road is

A new fright

But if I persevere

One day my

Mind may

Clear

Then I'll know

The things

That

Made me scream

Are nothing more

Than childish fears

That only look real

In bad dreams

These Words I Bleed for You

Pieces of my soul
Pour onto a page
For everyone to dissect
And analyze
Some people I know
Wear their hearts
On their sleeve
My Heart I keep in a pen
When I open my notebook
My heart bleeds
Words for you
A gentle whisper on your lips
Snapshots of my mind
So, you can know
The meaning of life
That I see

Triumphing Truth

Black mambas
Dancing at my feet
Faster and faster
The dust spirals and spins
Converging on truth
The emptiness of lies
Angels on a pins head
And camels in the needles eye
Flesh resists
But nature wins

Typewriter Monkeys

There's an infinite number
Of monkeys in my head
Sitting in front of typewriters
An infinite number of those too
The monkeys they type
And they type some more
Trying to write the next great novel
No not that
They're not interested in literature
Just the bananas
They get
At the end of the day

Unconscious Process of Thought

Regurgitated love
Symbioses has ended
Fidelity
Never was
Chakras clogged
From misuse
Too much heat
Has burned my soul
The facade finally
Crumbles
The truth is
Now exposed
Energy conflicts
Heart never touched
Lust for passion
Appearance deceived
Preconditioned
Cultural beliefs
How can I trust?
Love has lied to me

Unfolds

Hands gliding...over...
the keyboard...typing...
words...
making sentences...
then...paragraphs...
a story...
unfolds...
on a... glowing...
Screen...

Untitled 1

Peculiar softness
Fortuitous flip out
Exemplify hard
The expansive
Region that can't be defined
Patterns of colors
Mental filter
Emotional reasoning
Cluttered and sumptuous

Untitled 2

Drawing sustenance
From the abyss
Like an infant
Sucking on a tit
I am the answer
Just not the chosen one

Untitled 3

Vented freedom
Dripping puss
Like a leaky valve
While the pressure
In my brain
Continues to build
Forcing me to spew words
With venomous intent

Utopia

Walk a maze,
to find the truth.
Where do I hide?
When the light shines,
too bright in my eyes.
Smell the scent,
of the coming day.
Trapped in my mind.
With no way out,
but to DIE!
Help me as I scream,
silently to be six feet below.
A headstone for comfort and rest,
will greet me there.
Suppressing self-hate.
It becomes too hard.
I pray for the end.
As I put the barrel in my mouth.

Utopia 2.0

The scene must be set
for maximum impact
The chair is placed
so, the next to come in
Will open the door
my corpse in plain view

On my CD player
is my favorite song
How can I laugh tomorrow
when I can't even smile today
Pictures of family
I cut off all their faces
Then place them around me
a shrine to the life that I hate
The shotgun
I place that under my chin
One last step,
an end to the pain

Wait

Wait...
Wait...
Wait...
Just a little longer
Before something happens
Something's got to happen right
When I don't know
Do you think it'll be soon
No, I think I'm going to
Have to wait just a little longer
Maybe
No not now
Stop thinking about it
A watched something
Never....
I forgot,
Oh well, I might remember latter.
When something happens.
Will I still be here?
I hope so.
Boils never boils
And it's a pot

Waiting for Dawn

Night
cold dark
rainy wet
sitting in doorway
hope waits for dawn
not too long
cardboard dry
a little comfort
plastic trash bags
wrapped about
wear to keep dry
a blade in
my pocket
for safety
sleep eludes
cannot rest
must stay
awake
keep
my guard
to see
another
sunrise

Water Flows

Tasting the water
As it flows over all things
Both the high and the low

What Do You See?

What do you see
When you look at am?
Am I just another homeless junkie?
Motherfucker don't you know
I got rid of that monkey
Or doesn't that shit matter to you
Maybe you think it's true
That once an addict
Always an addict
But the only pills
That I take today
Are the ones I've been told
Will fix my fucking head
I don't care what you say
I'm not mentally dead
Do you want to take my brain
And dissect it?
Yeah, I'm still homeless
What's it to you?
You don't know my story
Look at me
Fucking look at me
What do you see?
I'm your future asshole
If you don't watch your back
Don't think it can happen to you?
Get real motherfucker
Just one bad choice
Is all it takes
You'll go from dinning on steaks

To eating out of trashcans
Don't you see
The only difference
Between you and me
Is that one bad choice
But I still have my voice
And I'll tell you the truth
The fucking truth I see
There isn't any difference
Between you and me

Words End

With pen in hand
I can conquer anything
But why do I want
To write without words
Words they seem
To limit what I say
They pigeonhole ideals
And trap ideals

Particle Dreams Thank You

Moore in space sat inside us.
And guess what all the species do...
Once the sun slips from the panel
And star dust expands inside our gut.
Merlin, ugh, never ever attend space.
The sun's not all we are to them...
Well maybe more, to know them.
Don't tell fairy tales.
'Cause that's not what you're taking as a green light.
'Til we're outside the hearth, all the way.
And the others have already got dug the tunnel out...
A region
The sky is blue.
I want to travel there.
The starry sky
We cannot stand beneath the highest of the mountain.
It's the children of the world.
Approach and embrace from below.
I see the destruction.
And why should we not...
A friend wishes for forests and birds to only smile happy like
Just a touch bit
I'm not one to cry under rain.

What is the walking?

What's really there.
The memories of here
What's in your mind?
What's outside your mind?
Particle dreams
Drifting into tangent
And swirling around a Crystal Bowl
Can't really tell.
No pattern, it's all ours
To know where we came from
To untangle the very fabric
Pictures waiting to pierce the veil.
So myriad images within swirling images
Photos, video they are.
Mills of ever-changing forms.
Spinning, spinning, spinning away
Storytelling, stories, stories
All of it all inside you
Babies start and fire off missiles.
Life forms take flight.
Or run to dance with Daddy,
And I get off it.
If I get off it, it's my own damn fault.
If I get off it, watch and learn.
What's inside our heads?
All in your head thousand dark pages
So, everything is in your head.
A million light years outside the curtain
This piecing together

How to Be a Butterfly

The brothers wake me up.
And this new life begins.
We are all a part of one.
The sun begins to rise.
And stops trembling.
The wind ceases to roar.
Death's clouds close
You and I have come to Earth.
Within our cracks and crevices
This is the new place.
Sentient creatures soon begin to awaken.
Branches & ladders are breaking up.
Lovely creatures steel oneself against the flowering
The filaments of their bodies
Incandescent, we'll step forth.
Now I'm a butterfly and
Flying within the wind I find
Something very alive and warm
The wind and my wings
Creaks wake me up again.
A single light shines from the dawn.
The sun remains lashing.
Its fall upon the night and that I begin my wings.
I see a weird light.
A tiny bubble starts to make.
The light grows to suck up the roof.
The bubble pops, exposing the dreams in my head.
My father lies during a pool of water.
Cracked into pieces by cosmic rays.
Exploding chunks of drool

Fall faster from the sky.
I hear a voice in my mind.
Tonight, I'm a computer, not a man.
You are what you wanted to be.
A butterfly sits on a flower's petals.
The brain sleeps at a trillion monitors.
Drowning in an infinite sea of pixels
Reality, the whole universe, a vertical beach
A rainbow may be a color that stands call at my eyes.
But you'll freeze time and fate.
Where you're and forget everything
Spell alphabet words with slow, slow patches
What's your name?
It is dumb and that I want to find out.
It is still fully cry out for a solution.
In full cry out for a solution it isn't my job to inform you who you're
In this sense, you'll never learn to be anything.
But from over the horizon
I see a star so brilliant.
A star during a sea of mists and blues
A star calling me here, does one hear?
You are what you would like to be.
A butterfly sits on a flower's petals.
The brain sleeps at a trillion monitors.
Drowning in an infinite sea of pixels
Reality, the whole universe, a vertical beach
A rainbow may be a color that stands call at my eyes.
But you'll freeze time and fate.
Where you're and forget everything
Spell alphabet words with slow, slow patches
The sound of something fluttering within the wind...
Your shoes come off, they're overlarge.

A man during a mask of white sombreros leaps from an airplane
He lights a cigarette, looks at the camera.
He looks around, seems pitying an equivalent thing.
He stands within the middle of the bottom.
And he takes a puff from his cigarette.
It fits his shoes and fits him snugly.
The shadow behind him is as solid as a mountain.
By this point I've only began your shirt
But I forbid you to ask my name first.
I am your daughter and you cannot betray me.
I'm afraid to allow you to skills I felt.
I have been to your school; I have been to your church.
I asked the teachers, the creeps, what was the purpose.
They whispered it wasn't my fault.
These are the dreams that I used to be raised to fear.
You have fallen into hell and now you'll enjoy it.
Your lips are arched, and you create a face.
Poker face, you think that you're funny.
Evil grin, you duck anytime the pale of eyes don't.
You bent right down to devour your toys, couldn't avert your eyes.
A giant skull and an enormous foot
It's all you recognize; you act sort of a child.
And I'm pretty sure you recognize what you're doing.
The earthquake has reached our world.
But nothing will change.
The death of the individual will only bring.
A new, insane world once we separate.
And albeit what you've done is one small a part of that new existence
I'm curious and that I can understand the impulse.
And why you'd wish to listen to this.
If my name is Jacob and you have slain me, too?

The magick

The magick grows stronger as its power
Grows crueler because it becomes more
Of an illusion itself
At the last moment the needs disappear
And we come to understand
That as we fall asleep into the night
Our dreams are quietly drowned in sound
The Tangle itself you see within the distance

The Golden bottle

No fae want to break down no fairies didn't!
The preparation starts.
The bottle of mead is poured!
Does it really need to be dark?
To the Moon
We watched the moon rise.
over the air surrounding the remainder of the planet
It was too beautiful a sight.
yet it brought with it the smell of lavender.
...and the sound of babbling brooks.
And the night air
But we've lost our way.
And it doesn't appear to be we'll ever find it again.
And the watchman has lost his light.
With each step, we've become doubly lost.
Naming the celebs turns down the sunshine.
And we've lost our bright place.
The stars 'light 'luminosity is gone now.
And it looks like we'll never find it.
And the nights are not any longer as lonely as they once were.
And so, I counsel the guts to stay beside the new actually.
Is that where the moon is as well?
Heavier in the dark the trail is formed harder.
And so, I gaze in wonder at the sun on the front.
And the water on the top
The grass shining large.
And the waters blue.
Just a touch further along the trail
The path grows longer.
With every curve during a pale glow

The gods have always given it their support.
Our help they've always offered sometimes.
When it appeared to defeat all hope
And it seems nobody saw it coming.
There was a force in situation.
To mold the planet into any shape we'd like.
And it appeared to come again permanently.
Dance within the Milky Way
I used to be making my mind up about.
watching out for Zephyrus (Mother Nature)
so, I wrote the lines:
The seats of Oar and House were lost in mist,
but their hands still held the drum.
Endowing at their sides winged children of sun and thunder.
But now they're becoming ghosts and flies buzz about the seats.
Mountains and valleys fall by the endless star's night and day.
Leaves their powder and mud and blots our roads.
That light leaving our perishable forests.
Sprawling across the land but lacking a transparent run
And our sounds get darkened in majesty.
'Til she sings the melody of her own lullaby
And walks around the precious place a European princess.
Wonders visiting and strange weeds flowing.
Fragrant vines smelling sweet from ages past.
It was some wonder that when lived within the garden.
at tree height still lying down smelling of honeysuckle
And some wonder that when lived within the garden at summers
grace.
And some wonder that when breathed during a dream of magnolias
tassel-like.
While their lively heart beating within the innocent night

Surrounded by meanings the foremost beautiful sides faced one
another.
An arrangement that defies the planet and stays where you're who are
looking for some happiness.
Working within the Grey Spaces
Yeah right as soon as I started scripting this song.
I knew I needed to urge it off my chest.
and that I ended up writing it during a few different tempos.
but I made a decision to end this one off.
because I felt just like the longer it visited the top,
the more I felt like I connected with this song more.
the primary time I actually played this song it made my skin crawl.
and froze me solidly in situation sort of a Pokémon that's long ago
been frozen.
it is the feeling of being stuck somewhere and nobody is.
in a position to seek out how out until you suddenly
desire you've got the facility to flee by simply committing to a specific
position.
it is a tough feeling but so worthwhile. No more nothin' brute force
here
I started at balance.
But I´m here still
When you mean to scream...
Smart, yet clumsy
Where every sound is delicacy.
That you can determine where you substitute this dance
Of worlds meeting together.
And it is time to place an end to the present dance.
Which goes on forever.
"The Golden Number" After writing everything else, my head was
spinning.
and that I was able to hand over.

Then I noticed this song could probably be a really good theme for a
Flash comic.
There just goes without saying, I'm getting to go attempt to make.
this a reality and see how it works.
The Doomed Rock
on behalf of me this song may be a declaration of my life
and therefore, the amount of your time since my divorce.
This song brought tears to my eyes and filled my heart with
gratitude for what I've been ready to achieve despite the important
life problems.
I affect all the time.
Now my life exposes with new possibilities.

The moon

The sensation of dying.
Now the moon sends on behalf of me only to go away me.
To die a drone in some sylph's belly.
When you cobble up the symphony of thy months
You outlast the days.
Those whose history it had been to face gazing at thee.
The nightingale who toils to craft a song siren.
Wades through forsaken seas,
Discarded cities, and weather of sighs.
Fine men without bronze at their breasts,
Courageous warriors without strength in their bones.
And when the sunrise set within the vast houses of cities
Their brightly shining exploits
The things men could name,
They now are the items men don't name.
I have been scared of death all my life.
And I have thought all the souls who died before me.
Might be a touch disturbed.
So, I even have set a trap1 for the lads.
Kicking them with my endless nails,
Still pounding on their chests
To show how tired and useless they're.
It's in fact one person taunting another.
A tangled shroud of fates to be pulled apart.
And my bowels are held hostage.
Unaccustomed to their presence,
I was so despondent.
To think they were all still alive.
I was shaken and frustrated by having to reload the shells.
I am also very thirsty and I'm sure there are other things.

That attend making that episode feel like such a waste.
Another, secret river, which washes into many a river dying.
Takes water from all frogs and birds and fish.
Man's underground if only to scrub away loathing the taste behind.
Remember that we are all one.

Ismael S. Rodriguez Jr. is a writer, poet, artist, and origami artist. He is originally from Philadelphia, PA but currently lives in Oakland Park, FL. He is a U.S. Navy veteran who served during Desert Storm. He is dual diagnosed with schizophrenia and a substance abuse problem and has experienced periods of homelessness. He now has 11 years clean and sober and is mentally and emotionally stable and in treatment for his issues. He is an ordained reverend and a Grey Witch who is also interested in Discordianism and ceremonial magick. He has a website where he posts poems, origami, and other things. The website is at bulletproofpoet.com[1] that link as well as other links can be found at https://allmylinks.com/mrizzy.

---

1. https://bulletproofpoet.com/